A POETRY BOOK

MELANCHOLIES OF MIDNIGHTS

ANISHA GOSWAMI

First Published in March 2023

ISBN: 978-93-5741-018-2

BLUEROSE PUBLISHERS

www.BlueRoseONE.com

info@bluerosepublishers.com

+91 8882 898 898

Cover Design:

Vibhuti Verma

Typographic Design:

Namrata Saini

Distributed by: BlueRose, Amazon, Flipkart

ACKNOWLEDGMENT

I could have not undertaken this journey without my parents, that blue and green diary, and the brown donut pen. My parents have always supported and encouraged my writing. There were times when I doubted if what I was writing was any good and each and every time, they were there to tell me that as long as I wrote what I truly wanted to write, it would be worth more than anything I'd ever own. I don't think I'd be publishing this book if it weren't for my mother who pushed me to take this step and I am so thankful to her for her determination and faith in me. I am ever more thankful to my father whose faith and confidence in me has never faltered and even more thankful for that smile he wears with his eyes when he feels proud of me because that brings such relief and comfort to my heart. A special mention to my younger brother for being a constant source of joy in my life.

I am grateful for the blue diary where I wrote my first poem in 2019 with the donut pen gifted to me by a dear friend. I am also thankful to that senior who wrote so well and the one by whom I was inspired to begin writing in the first place. I'd also like to express my gratitude to my friends who always listened to my poems and encouraged me to never stop writing.

Thank you. Thank you so much.

ACKNOWLEDGEMENT

DEDICATION

To the moon and sun, mom and dad, that are the reason I made it through the melancholies of midnights and mornings.

PREFACE

A poetry book of thoughts, feelings, and emotions that were never said. Of feelings and emotions that were never properly expressed. Feelings of unexplainable sadness, the struggle of masking that pain, wanting help yet refusing it, being lost yet wanting to find yourself. Of finally embracing the darkness enough to adjust one's eyes to have been able to see the light.

This book has been divided into 4 sections, each a stage of the journey so far. However, it is essential to note that even though the stages are expressed in chronological order, it isn't always so. In a journey, it is possible and quite alright to go back to certain stages or even skip a couple. A journey of anything is far from linear and consistent. I find myself at the 4th stage at the moment yet I do not fear the possibility of having to experience the preceding stages again.

My mother says I am an old soul, I don't know much about that so for the lack of a better word, I'll call it empathy. My empathy, whose origin I do not know, has given me the chance to feel more emotions and feelings apart from my own. A lot of the topics I've written about have been inspired by said empathy. Yet being able to perceive others' pain and yet not being able to help make it any less makes you, yourself, feel hopeless and lost and causes feelings of stress and depression. Being able to perceive others' pain itself becomes a pain. And the inability to verbally express the mess in one's head makes it even harder.

After writing my first poem, I felt lighter and it felt easier to understand everything. The mess of emotions and feelings in my head felt organized through writing the poems. And I remember reading poems and feeling a sense of being found, of being understood, and of finding relief in the fact that I was not alone. And so I hope that someone can feel the same through reading my poems.

Because we've all had moments and periods of time in our life when we've felt as if we've been submerged in complete darkness. We've felt feelings of depression, anxiety, hopelessness, and melancholy. This book tangibly gives a voice to those emotions, feelings, and intrusive thoughts. Acknowledging their realness and impact on our lives yet also understanding that they're of transient nature. Understanding that it is possible to let go of such burdening emotions, that it is possible to stop others and our own selves from pushing us down, that it is possible to let go all the while remembering that this too shall pass.

This too shall pass.

ABOUT THE AUTHOR

Anisha Goswami is an 18-year-old writer, poetess, singer, and law aspirant. Overcome with a passion for writing, Anisha initially started her writing journey in the US, where she lived for 4 years. She properly started writing poems at the age of 13 and has so far written more than 100 poems. Her poems not only reflect her own emotions but most often than not express the various struggles and experiences of people, both people around her and afar.

She believes in giving a voice to your thoughts, both the bad and the good, to find a sense of realness in a world where everything so often feels unreal, in an attempt to validate your thoughts and see them tangibly enough to have the strength to overcome them. Anisha hopes that her words and poems can help readers feel less alone during the melancholies of midnights.

Anisha wrote M.O.M as an attempt to verbalize through words the struggles, thoughts, and emotions of people who aren't able to voice their pain and inner, and outer battles out loud. She hopes that M.O.M can help said individuals feel more validated and less alone in their journey.

Anisha was nominated for Author of the year 2022 by India's #1 Literature Platform, StoryMirror. Anisha cleared CLAT 2023 with an AIR 1429 and an MP Rank of 80. She currently has a writing page on Instagram, @a_rxsepxtals, where she shares poems, prose, oneliner, etc. Anisha lives with her parents and younger brother in Bhopal.

CONTENTS

1. Bare Beginnings

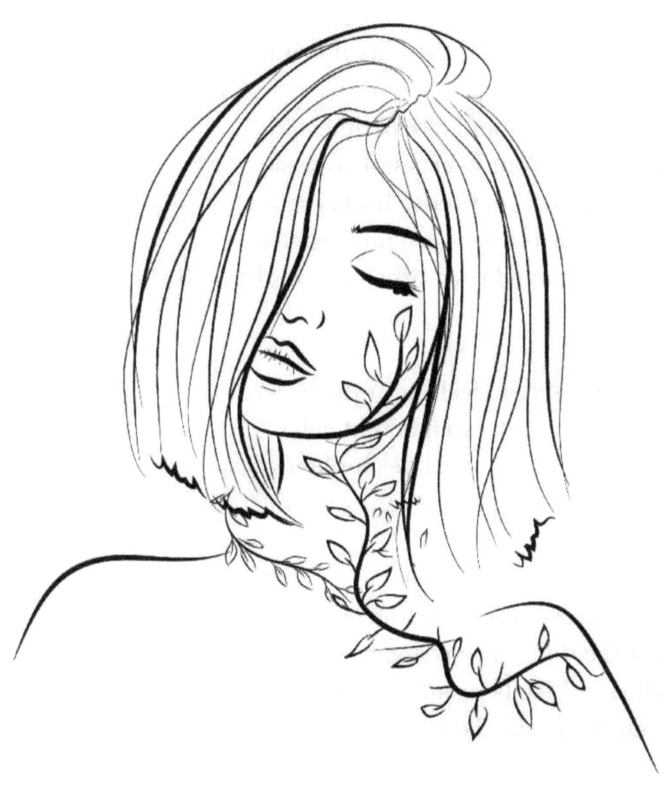

1. The sky that bleeds

The sky bleeds in violet
Pink clouds discolor
As they bandage to cosset
Unhealed secrets, the hurt murmurs

Galaxy as big and old as time
Yet benevolent hearts not so wise
Still, the sky and those hearts relate
Both their burdens are unweighted
To understand each other, the night is all that is needed

An eerie serene feeling in the heart
Because it understands that ache
Of being so beautiful yet broken apart
Perhaps giving too much is the mistake

In the hush of the dusk
The heart finds a kindred spirit above
Yet the difference is apparent enough
The sky bleeds proudly with dignity
Something this heart never does

- Anisha G.G

(Illustration by Vibhuti Verma)

2. Tears of Gasoline

Mind's gears twist and turn
Chains hold like metal fetters
The engine of my feelings runs
With fuel and toxic letters

The meter goes over the limit
Overwhelming speed of thoughts
But I'm exhausted In just minutes
Left stranded nowhere, joyous distraught

Alone yet still with myself
What is this, a body or a machine?
Hot and heating, I'm overwhelmed
We both cried tears of gasoline

– Anisha G.G

3. Coffee

These thoughts are bitter
Bitter badly like coffee
Could tears water me down? I consider
(Dilute these emotions in her?)

Its smell is so familiar
A sort of warmth like an old friend
It gives a nightmarish nostalgia
Good and bad I suppose it is

Yet in my mind, it brews hot
This anger, and frustration brews
There is no sugar. None at all
The coffee is ready. So are my daily rues

Biscuits and a breakdown
How conventional?
In a sea of caffeine, I drown
Perhaps I'm too emotional?

Lost in my world as it all pipes down
I forget to drink too
Now the coffee is cold, and I frown
Because I am cold too.

Breezing cold and heartless
Blue sadness. And then I empty it down
It's still bitter in its coldness
But easier to drink like expired poison

I drink till the very last drop
Perhaps when vehement, again shows up
Let's have another coffee date
When shall we have another cup?

- Anisha G.G

(Illustration by Vibhuti Verma)

4. Drunk on Tears

I Don't mind getting hurt
I'm addicted to pain
My thoughts open my mind apart
To intoxicate the already intoxicated brain

Am I an alcoholic of feeling melancholic?
Too dazed on these despairs
How much am I supposed to drink?
When I'm already to the brink
Drunk on tears

- Anisha G.G

5. Tears or Rain?

My eyes feel as heavy
As those rain-filled clouds above
Weighing down to bury
These teardrops that aren't enough

The heaviness colors them dull
Like a water-soaked cotton
I absorb the pain to feel less null
Are they drops of tears or rain? I have forgotten

(I am never alone in august, the sky cries with me)

- Anisha G.G

6. Poisonous Medicine

The darkness embraced me
When I was alone with my thoughts
Its cold hands wrapped around me
To give comfort and warmth

I felt at a perfect peace
As everything seemed right and that was odd
How could hurting myself be my medicine
I wondered a lot

- Anisha G.G

7. The Unwanted Guests

As the doorbell rings
My heart starts going up and down the stairs
As it knows what this call brings
As it knows it's the unwanted pairs

More than my eyes
My heart cries
It fears, what's coming next
And so, it timidly tears
As it welcomes the unwanted guests

Depression and anxiety are their names
They invade the heart that is your home
And mischievously play a very mean game
2-1, you are made to lose alone

They tell me "We're here for you," don't worry
That I do not need anyone else
They are here to stay, there is no hurry
(Pat. Pat.) So, Do I even need myself?

Like weeds and vines, they grow
With their need to take over, expressed
In my blood, weed killers flow to only kill me though
It slowly feels like I am becoming the guest

- Anisha G.G

8. My heart's sound: Acoustic anxiety

The walls are walking too close towards me
The clock is tick talking
And its hum like a slowed, reverbing laugh of mocking

Because time is dripping away like wastewater
But in my heart, nothing is of grave matter

Yet sometimes everything does matter
Even the things that aren't supposed to matter
I'm stuck in a limbo
Between doing bright or letting my life tatter

My heart beats to warn that I am still alive in this place
Yet that warning is nothing but useless care
A reminder that reminds me why I forgot to live in the first place

A fast-paced dance to a slow song
And my feet just love kissing the ground
I stand still and dizzy to the prancing world
But I have my own rhythm to dance to called "My heart's sound"

- Anisha G.G

2. Mayday Masks

1. Hateful Love

I hear so many voices
With the same frequency
Crack and hiss, static noises
like a radio in my head

But I tune out the beautiful songs
To listen to the nonsense noise, frequently
And the hours are short yet long
In self-loathing and discrepancy

But the hate resonates louder
Than the vibrations of love
Because I think I deserve
to hear nothing but hateful love

- Anisha G.G

2. Who's Better to Judge Me Than Me?

I look at the mirror and heave a sigh
Every part of me I take in and revile
To the voices in my head, I comply
Wiping my tears, I put on a smile

I can feel their scrutinizing eyes
Analyzing every deep detail
But of course, not more than the eyes
Of the inner dark demon

So, to become better, I'll strive
Every drop of blood and tear devoted
But before the start, intrusion arrives
And I lose all mere motivation

I fight the war inside my head
The voices I try to ignore
I work myself till I feel dead
Nothing I do feels enough, though

Yet again, by nightfall
I am back to the start
Surprisingly, louder are the calls
More brain-twisting the songs

I, again, look at the mirror
Sullen and somber, I heave a sigh feeling empty
"I'll never be free", I let out a cry and decide
Knowing Who is better to judge me than me?

- Anisha G.G

3. Pointlessly Valid

Finding myself in the sea
Of endless thoughts
Finding the balance on the beam
While untangling the knots

Finding the things to adjoin
With a sick feeling of striving and strife
A pointless point to finding the point
To this meaningless life

- Anisha G.G

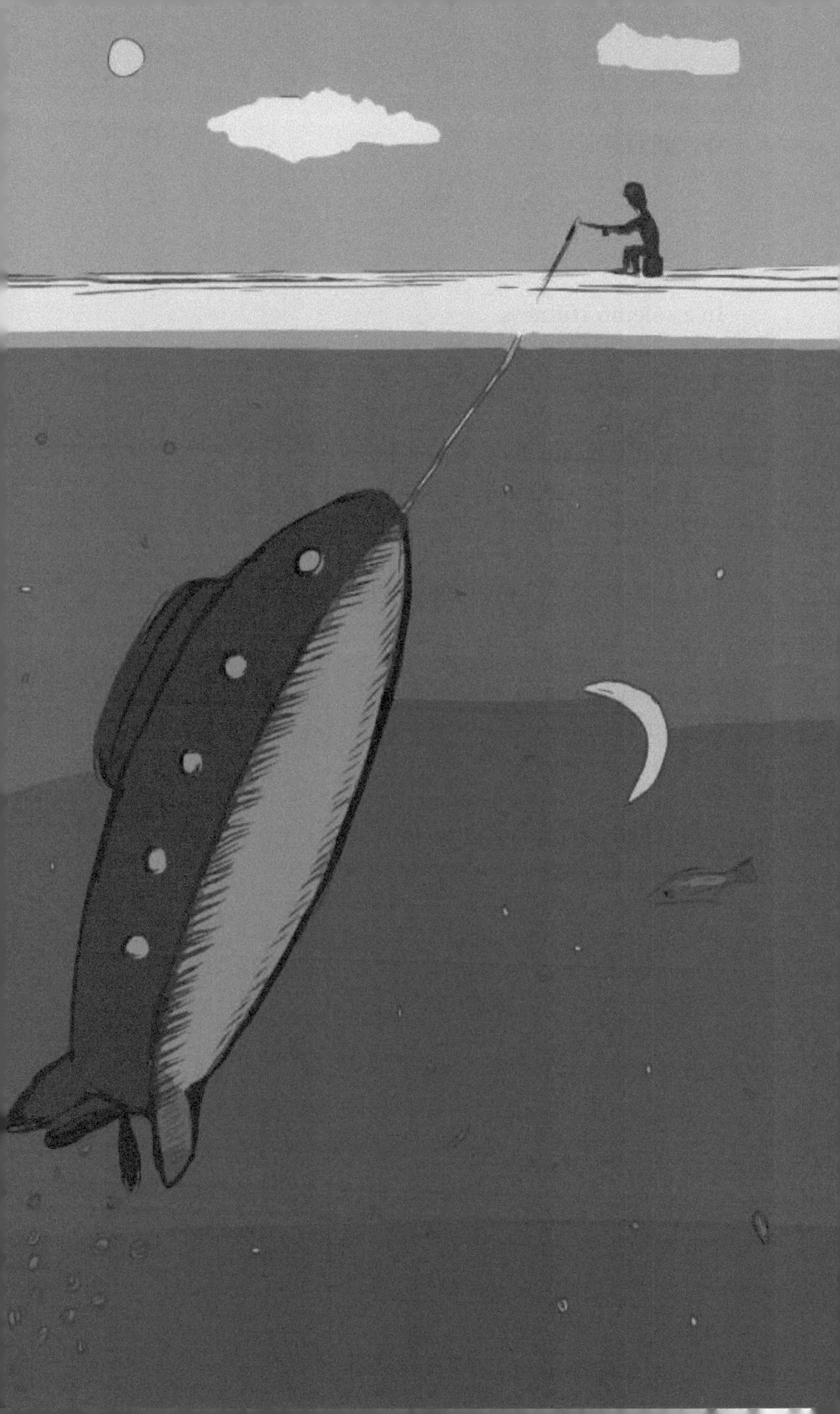

4. Still

In a solemn stillness
My mind has frozen
Yet the world is about

I look at the cars
And all I can see is how still they are
And I look at myself
Where my mind has parked itself
In a solemn state of unintelligible despair

Where my heart has parked itself
In a dusty no-place garage
Of heartache that has no wound, to begin with,

I have chosen spots of suffering
Like a damned schadenfreude
But I am feasting upon my own misfortune

These cars, they are alone in their idleness
Objects with a strict purpose to yield usefulness
And my *objects* are no different, are they?

Is it something I've culminated from my own actions
Or is this something everybody has become or becomes
And I just happen to be an unfortunate soul
Bored enough to ponder upon the meaning of it all?

When there is no meaning to existence
Rather than the mere act of existing itself
At the end of it all.

- Anisha G.G

5. Am I Valid?

Am I valid?
Are these the pieces of a puzzle never meant to be solved
Or the rings to that final helpless call

Am I valid?
To have the right to feel what I feel
Despite having everything I could and could not have

Am I valid?
Even if there are millions in the dark like me
And some in worse despair than I could ever see

Am I valid?
Do I not have a right to try and fail and not be able to get up?

Am I valid?
Because I feel like I don't have enough problems to have the right to be sad.
Because I feel like I don't have enough proof and validity
to show that I am *not* okay

So, I ask
Am I enough. Am I valid enough to not be okay?

- Anisha G.G

6. Hide

She wanted them to ask
She wanted them to ask
But when they did
She put on a mask

- Anisha G.G

7. Paint My Face

The colors bloomed in vibrancy
As she stood among the crowd
But they threatened to leave in urgency
As she spent more time around

A painting of a black sky
With weary white clouds
Covered her features as she returned inside
Then bloomed an eerie sense of proud

- Anisha G.G

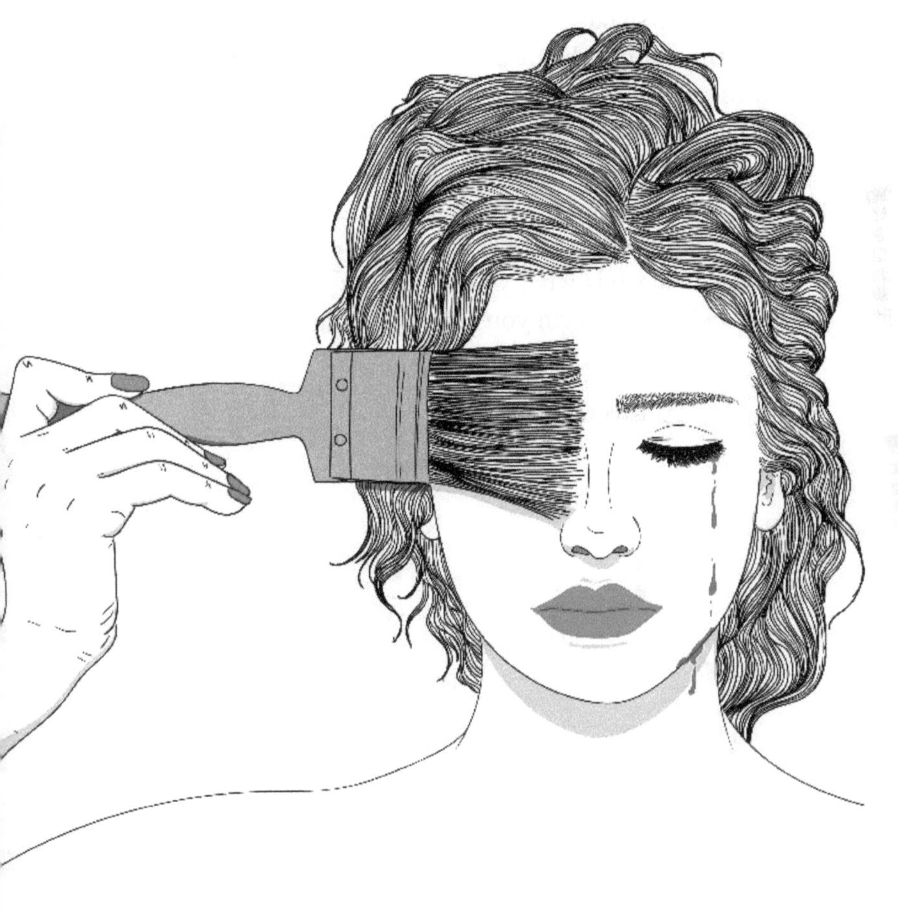

8. All I Can Not Say

My hands shake as the words spill out of my mouth
But the reality, the medium of speech, is left screaming in the mind
When all that does come out is salty tears and choked sobs

And reality is a nightmare you're living
Peace in sleep is what you're craving
Yet help is an alarm you keep snoozing

- Anisha G.G

3. Forgotten farewells

1. Quiet

I stayed quiet
The weight of my thoughts
Not only burdened my mind
But weighed down on my lips
Bang! Shutting them shut
Shut and stuck like a jammed door

Perhaps like a paperweight
On a piece of paper
If you tear paper, nothing full can be written
Neither can torn lips go beyond whispers

Creaks and sighs, wrinkles, and cries
But no words Escape, none of real significance
anyways.
Reality is rather trapped, helplessly, inside my throat
I stayed quiet

and I will stay quiet
For even after the weight is gone
For I will have forgotten how to talk

- Anisha G.G

2. There are days

There are days
When I feel empty like a dug-out grave
Just waiting for something to be filled in
Even if it's death

But not pain
Please I have had enough of that
No hurt. No no.
I've seen enough people be unhappy and hurt

There are days
When I can feel my eyes dry
Hollow from crying too much
yet not crying enough

There are days
When my heart aches so much
It feels like the cages will break
from the force of the earthquake of my heart
It aches so much that my left shoulder hurts
And I feel like my whole body will fall apart

There are days Like the above
Where my room is filled with silence
And though I breathe out loud
My sighs scream in pain
And I know my soul has stopped

- Anisha G.G

3. Dusty old souls

There was dust on her heart
She hadn't loved in a long time
There was dust on her feelings
She hadn't felt in a long time
There was dust on her soul
She hadn't been alive for a while

- Anisha G.G

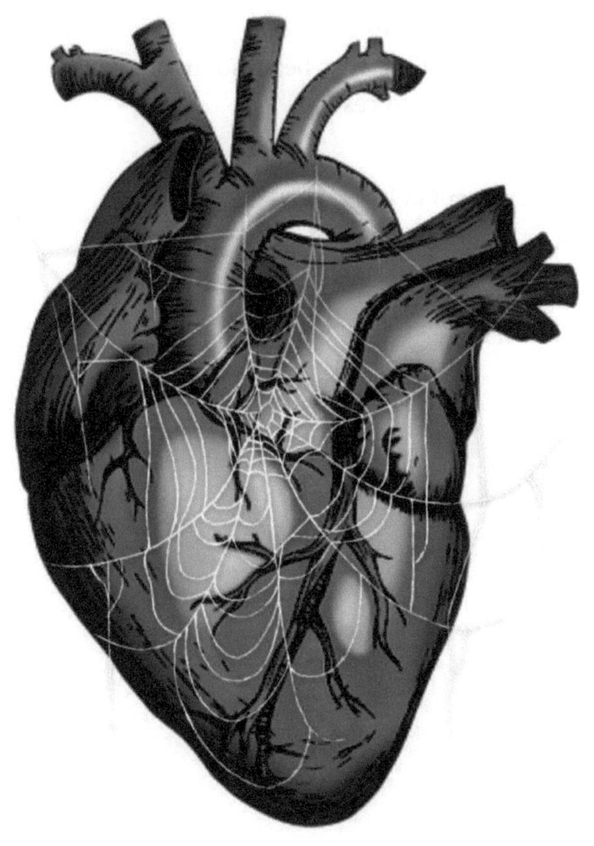

4. And I'll rip my own heart out

And I rejoice in this heartache
For it gives me hope
That this little thing that beats so involuntarily
Might finally get to rest

- Anisha G.G

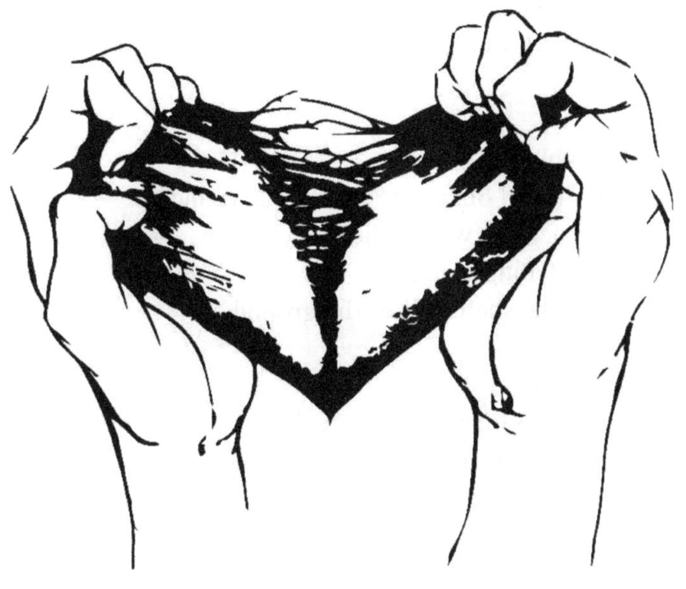

5. The Table

I look at the table
While on a chair, I sit
Feeling so unstable
And melancholy with thoughts of things I could commit

On the table
Seen is a metal object, with six little rounds
Want to neglect with a click
And a deafening sound
Through the shells fall to the ground.

On the table
A necklace to lift me above the land
A polymer rope, a copper wire, a cable
Let's lose at the game of hangman!

On the table
A container full of candies
To make me sweat and give a sugar crush
But surely, they come in handy
To stop life and its chaotic rush

On the table
A pack of sharp metallic crayons
My body starts to feel like a page
Let the reds be filled in
This masterpiece can never be erased

So many ways to leave
An exit, an escape they enabled
Not easy but at last they do relieve
I wonder as I look at the table

My soul flying away
Mind and heart disabled
I committed into this love and I lay
Not on or at, but by the table

(Lips tight, eyes closed, last breath)
(Away and away, lie dead by the table)

- Anisha G.G

6. What Weather!

The light bulb of the storm
Reigns The dark sky over
Flickering and crackling in its form
It is more overused than broken moreover

The pain flows out in blood
From the very veins
The pain flows out in a flood
From the very rain

For that very Same reason they share
The heart and the sky cry together
And the world exclaims "What weather!."

- Anisha G.G

(Illustration by Vibhuti Verma)

7. Remnants

I can see the remnants of my old self
Peeking through the windows of my mind. Knocking at the door, they stand
Hoping to see if that part of me is still alive

- Anisha G.G

4. Heavy Healings

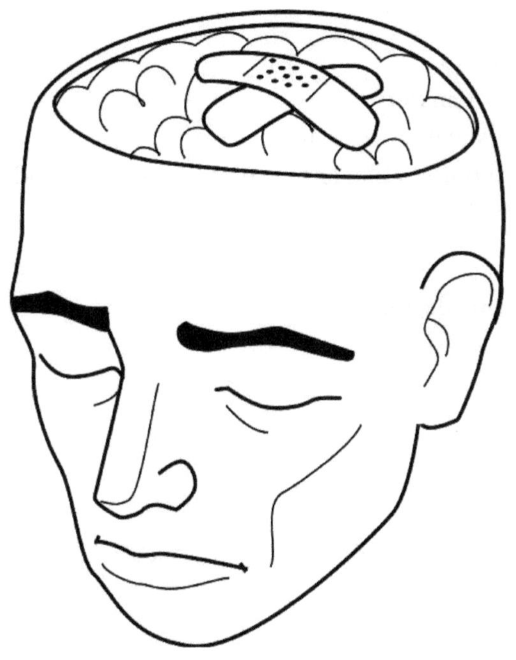

1. Free of what

And I long to be free.
Not of society
Or of worldly absurdities

But rather
of my own anxiety
Of unreasonable necessities
And of thoughts like fetters that adorn like necklaces
on my body

- Anisha G.G

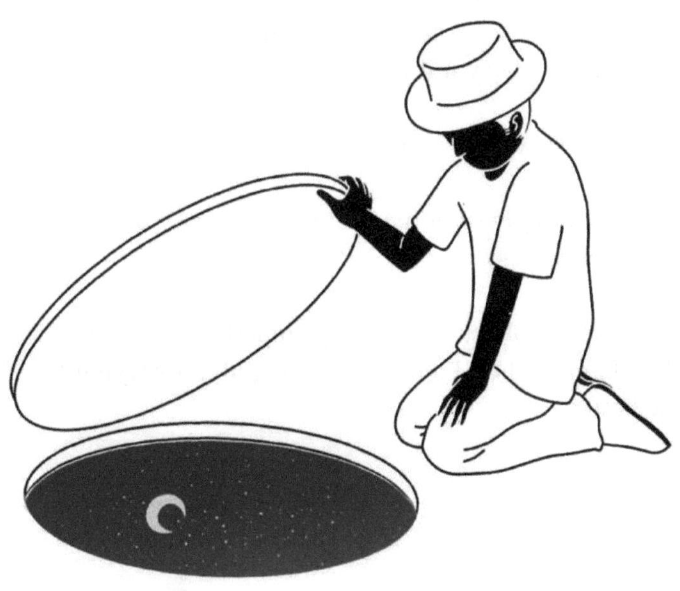

2. Convicted

I'm convicted of violence and instigation
Of violence and intimidation towards my own heart
For I've attacked it for its emotional tendencies and threatened to dry it if it worked too hard

It's a court session in my mind every day and every night
Yet I fail to give a proper judgment of guilt or innocence every time

Absolve me of my sins, for my empathy is my fetter
For I am neither, I am innocently guilty for trying to be better

To myself now
In the only way I know how.

- Anisha G.G

3. Fading bearings

The events cemented in time
And you find yourself walking over them
Kneeling and tracing the curves and Edges of the marked happening like a deeply carved scar
Unforgiving in its power to stay etched in time

Some are smooth
And some are rough enough to reopen membranes of pain
You still trace them, unable to resist their presence

But In time, as you walk over them and dust your hands over them
They start to fade with wear and tear of acknowledging them too often and too much
The entire routine becoming too unfruitful
A sense forgiveness highlighting them and your heart

The carvings becoming ever so distant in your gaze
Yet still they exist. The depressions on the concrete will forever be there
But the burden of their bearings isn't that burdening anymore

- Anisha G.G

4. World of me

The world twinkled around me
I was the dark sky
So, these suns and stars grow
And I remain an oblivious mass of space

And although I am free
While they are bound to gravity
I do not have an aim, voided volatile flow
They eventually find a place

They are free of instability
Yet they are bound to the universe
I am the definition of instability
Yet I am my own universe

- Anisha G.G

5. Your self

Close your eyes, you tell
Don't look anywhere else
Just in your mind
You will find that missing piece
Is your self

- Anisha G.G

6. Life is a home of Yin and Yang

This sun is too blinding
From the window, it's too bright
This peace is too binding
From zero to hope, it's too frightening
This house is my home

That night was too real
Behind the closed doors of trouble
That despair was too reeling
Behind the smile, the pain was double
And maybe I was alone
But That was also my home

For so maybe I need to accept
This yin and yang of mind
Neither is to exempt
For I need both to survive

- Anisha G.G

7. Snowflakes

May your scars
Bloom into snowflakes
And may the kiss of winter
Provide you a reason to feel warm

(You deserve the love)

- Anisha G.G

(Illustration by Vibhuti Verma)

9 789357 410182

Printed by Libri Plureos GmbH in Hamburg, Germany